TAKING IT ALL BACK

T.J. MCBRIDE

ISBN-13: 978-0-578-98505-3

TJ McBride Ministries
P.O. Box 728
McDonough, Georgia 30253
www.tjmcbride.org

Printed in the United States of America.

First Edition: October 2021

CONTENTS

INTRODUCTION

It's time to take back everything the enemy has stolen and walk in total victory! There is a supernatural power of restoration available to you to recover all. No longer will you sit on the sidelines of your life, hoping that things will get better. Ephesians 2:6 says, "…and hath raised us up together, and made us sit together in heavenly places in Christ Jesus." When God raised Jesus, He raised you. When He seated Jesus, He seated you in Him. Ephesians 1:21 says that this seating is "far above all principality, and power, and might, and dominion, and every name that is named, not only in this world, but also in that which is to come."

You're not fighting for the victory but from a place of victory. This is why Paul called it the good fight of faith in his letter to Timothy. We are living in the end of days and on the brink of the closing of an age as we prepare for the second coming of Christ. The glory of God is going to rest on believers in the body of Christ like never before. We are going to be witnesses of His power and glory as He uses every willing and available member in the body of Christ to preach the Gospel and fulfill their heavenly assignments.

It's time to claim what is already yours! Psalm 23:5 says that He has prepared a table for you in the presence of your enemies. You've been standing long enough. It's time to attend the banquet, sit in your reserved seat, and partake of the provision of healing, deliverance, divine protection, victory, prosperity, peace, and clarity of direction on your next steps in the plan and will of God for your life.

When the plagues of Egypt came, the scriptures remind us that the covenant children of Israel were in the land of Goshen unaffected by the plague. They looked out from the covering of the secret place of God at the destruction that was coming upon the world. If you're in Egypt, you're in the wrong spot. It's time to adjust your coordinates and get to the land of Goshen, the place of divine covering from the antics and strategies of the devil.

This book is a testament to the power of God at work in my own life, as God has restored my family, my ministry, and my finances. When my wife, myself, and our children left San Francisco to start a church in Georgia, we had no idea the obstacles that would face us in obeying God. We've taken some hits as a family, but I'm standing today strong to declare that if God can turn it around for us, He will do the same for you. It's time to access the supernatural power of restoration! We're taking it all back!

CHAPTER ONE
The Power of Restoration

Joel 2:25-26
"And I will restore to you the years that the locust hath eaten, the cankerworm, and the caterpillar, and the palmerworm, my great army which I sent among you. And ye shall eat in plenty, and be satisfied, and praise the name of the Lord your God that hath dealt wondrously with you: and my people shall never be ashamed."

For far too long, many of us have lived beneath our rights and privileges as members of the body of Christ. We can see the plan of God clearly laid out in the scriptures for us to walk in total victory as sons and daughters of God. From the Old to the New Testament, we see men and women connecting, and at times, disconnecting from God's great plan. Victory has always been interwoven in this plan, and in any area where we have fallen short of receiving the fullness of our inheritance, there is an ever-present power ready to bring us into restoration.

Restoration is the return of something to an original or unimpaired condition. It is the restitution of something taken away or lost.[1] In the Garden of Eden, we see the original and intended state of man. According to Genesis 1:26, in the beginning, God made us in His image with His nature. We are a reflection of Him in the earth with His authority to rule and reign.

He created us to flourish in a state of wholeness and completeness, lacking nothing. Our mandate from God was to dominate, prosper, reproduce, and fill the earth. Let's take an ariel view through the lens of scripture of the original state of man in the Garden of Eden.

- He was crowned with God's glory and honor. There was no physical death or sickness and disease on the earth. (Genesis 1:26; Psalm 8:5-6)

- He had dominion over the works of God's hands. (Psalm 8:6)

- He had the mind and infinite wisdom of God displayed in his ability to name every animal in the animal kingdom. Man used 100% of his mental capacity, whereas we only use a fraction today. Notice that the Bible never records that Adam attended a school to learn mathematics, literature, science, language, or physics. He came into being with the life, nature, and mind of God. (Genesis 2:19-20)

- He had the spiritual capacity to perceive, receive, and fulfill the assignments of God. (Genesis 2:15)

- He had an unlimited provision in the Garden of Eden. A river went out of Eden to water the garden that divided into four rivers that led to gold, bdellium, and onyx stone. (Genesis 2:10 - 14)

• He had intimate fellowship and communion with God. This is evidenced by Adam and Eve's ability to sense the presence of God approaching them in the garden in the cool of the day. In God's presence, there was no lack, sense of guilt or inferiority, sickness, disease, confusion, depression, anxiety, or defeat. (Genesis 3:8)

Two groups were observing the creation and crowning of man: the angels and Satan. Notice the angels' observation here in Psalm 8:4-6, "What is man, that thou art mindful of him? And the son of man, that thou visitest him?...crowned him with glory and honor. Thou madest him to have dominion over the works of thy hands; thou hast put all things under his feet." Satan saw the creation of mankind as well and his dominion in the earth. He employed a strategy to steal, kill and destroy him and the plan of God.

Deception is an age-old strategy the enemy has been using since the beginning. It is a pathway that leads to the demise of one's ability to operate in dominion, as seen with Adam and Eve. The enemy purposely misled Eve by providing and suggesting misinformation to take an alternative path of disobedience that was different from the one God intended.

This is how he steals the victory in areas of our lives. Notice in Genesis 3:1-4, "...Yea, hath God said, Ye shall not eat of every tree of the garden? And the woman said unto the serpent, We may eat of the fruit of the trees of the garden: but of the fruit of the tree which is in the midst of the garden, God hath said, Ye shall not eat of it, neither shall you touch it, lest ye die. And the serpent said unto the woman, Ye shall not surely die:"

Do you see the deception and lies of the enemy in this passage of scripture? This is how he attacks us but thank God we don't have to be ignorant of his devices. The Bible reminds us in James 4:7 to resist the devil, and he will flee from us. We resist the devil by obeying the Word of God, commanding him to leave and take his hands off of every area of our life, pleading the blood of Jesus over what rightfully belongs to us, and declaring the promises of God.

If Adam and Eve had resisted the devil, he never would have gained access into their life, mankind, and all of creation. Their disobedience opened the door for the law of sin and death to enter into this earth realm. The law of sin and death is a law at work that produces sickness, disease, lack, confusion, and all works of evil.

Man died spiritually, which eventually led to physical death. However, this was not a part of God's original design.

Mankind was separated from God, dominion, authority, and provision. Romans 3:23 says, "for all have sinned, and come short of the glory of God." In essence, Adam and Eve fell from the glory of God that had been their garments in the garden. All of us were born into this fallen state (Romans 5:17). This fall from grace tainted the purpose God created us to fulfill. Emotional, physical, and spiritual turmoil followed this tragic event. As a result, we disconnected from the source that guides and represents all truth.

Thank God for the redemptive plan of God to bring us back into the right relationship with God and restore all that was lost. God sent Jesus to pay the penalty as the ultimate life sacrifice. "Yes,

Adam's one sin brings condemnation for everyone, but Christ's one act of righteousness brings a right relationship with God and new life for everyone" (Romans 5:18, NLT). This means we can live our lives whole, complete, and in total restoration.

Consider the prophet Joel's prophesy to the children of Israel. The Bible says the people had left the presence of God and become reliant on their ability to thrive. Leaving the presence of God will always disconnect us from the provision of God. As a result, they experienced famine and lack in the land. God reminds us in Isaiah 1:19 that if we are willing and obedient, we will eat the good of the land. It's time to get willing and obedient!

It's time to rightfully claim what belongs to us. Healing, deliverance, prosperity, peace, victory, and clarity are your rightful inheritance. Thank God, "Christ has redeemed us from the curse of the law, being made a curse of us: for it is written, Cursed is every one that hangeth on a tree: that the blessing of Abraham might come on the Gentiles through Jesus Christ; that we might receive the promise of the Spirit through faith" (Galatians 3:13-14). We are reminded in Romans 8:2 that the law of the Spirit of life in Christ Jesus has made us free from the law of sin of death. This law is greater and supersedes the residual effects in our life of the law of sin and death.

Tips for Restoration

- Renew your mind. Wrong thinking leads to wrong believing, which leads to actions and behaviors that work against restoration. Take time to renew your mind in these following areas: 1) who you are in Christ, 2) what rightfully belongs to you in Him, and 3) what you can do through Him.

- The New Testament epistles are a great starting place as it contains the Pauline revelation of the body of Christ. Take time to look up and meditate scriptures in the epistles with these phrases: 1) In Him; 2) By Him; 3) Through Him; 4) In Christ; 5) By Christ, and 6) Through Christ.

- A breakthrough in your restoration will be linked to your breakthrough in revelation, which fuels your faith. Meditation in the Word of God moves the Word from being information to revelation knowledge. It renews your mind and plants the Word in your heart so faith can arise. We are reminded in Romans 10:17 that faith comes by hearing the Word of God.

- Faith is the currency in the kingdom of God, like money is the currency in the natural realm. To take back everything the enemy has stolen, you're going to have to do it by faith. The foundation of your faith is revelation knowledge of God's Word.

I pray this book will cause the restorative power of God to operate in your life like never before. It is His will and desire that you take back everything the enemy has stolen. This time you're going to hold it and keep it resulting in perpetual victory. Your time of living up and down is over! It's time to climb, hold, and maintain your spiritual progress and advancement in the kingdom of God. This is the supernatural power of restoration!

Personal Reflection

1. What area(s) of your life need to be restored?

_____

_____

_____

_____

_____

2. Identify and list any open doors of disobedience (i.e., wrong thinking, wrong relationships, godly instructions that haven't been followed, etc.) that need to be closed so the redemptive work of restoration can begin.

_____

_____

_____

_____

_____

3. Locate and list below a scripture from the New Testament epistles that has one of the following phrases: 1) In Him; 2) By Him; 3) Through Him; 4) In Christ; 5) By Christ; 6) Through Christ. Spend the next twenty-four hours meditating on this scripture.

_____

_____

_____

_____

_____

Confession of Faith: I am restored in my health, finances, and relationships in Jesus' Name!

"

A BREAKTHROUGH IN
YOUR RESTORATION WILL
BE LINKED TO YOUR
BREAKTHROUGH IN
REVELATION.

"

CHAPTER TWO
Physical Restoration

Jeremiah 30:17
"For I will restore health unto thee, and I will heal thee of thy wounds, saith the Lord."

It is God's great desire to see us restored in divine health. Healing is your covenant right as a child of God. I'm reminded of the admonition in Psalm 23:5, "You prepare a table before me in the presence of my enemies..." Have you ever stopped and asked yourself what is on this table? There is a seat reserved for you, and healing is one of the meals the Father has prepared. Jesus paid the ultimate price so that the gift of healing would be your portion.

The scripture declares, *"But he was wounded for our transgressions, he was bruised for our iniquities: the chastisement of our peace was upon him; and with his stripes we are healed."* (Isaiah 53:5). The apostle Peter quotes directly from this passage in 1 Peter 2:24, *"who his own self bare our sins in his own body on the tree, that we, being dead to sins, should live unto righteousness; by whose stripes ye were healed."*

Let's take a moment and debunk any belief systems that may have led you to believe that healing is not God's will for you. The following are some powerful biblical truths with scriptural references to lay hold to by faith. Once you are healed, it's God's will that you move into divine health where you never experience sickness and disease in your body again.

Healing Belongs to You

- Isaiah 58:8 (AMPC), "Then shall your light break forth like the morning, and your healing (your restoration and the power of a new life) shall spring forth speedily…"
- Matthew 8:17, "that it might be fulfilled which was spoken by Esaias the prophet,

saying, Himself took our infirmities, and bare our sicknesses."

- Acts 10:38, "how God anointed Jesus of Nazareth with the Holy Ghost and with power: who went about doing good, and healing all that were oppressed of the devil; for God was with him."

Sickness & Disease Did Not Come From God

- John 10:10 (AMPC), "The thief comes only in order to steal and kill and destroy. I came that they may have and enjoy life, and have it in abundance (to the full, till it overflows)."

- James 1:13, "Let no man say when he is tempted, I am tempted of God: for God cannot be tempted with evil, neither tempteth he any man."

- James 1:17, "Every good gift and every perfect gift is from above, and cometh down from the Father of lights, with whom is no variableness, neither shadow of turning."

Healing Is Received by Faith

- Psalm 107:20, "He sent His word, and healed them, and delivered them from their destructions."

- Matthew 9:28-30, "And when he was come into the house, the blind men came to him: and Jesus saith unto them, Believe ye that I am able to do this? They said unto him, Yea, Lord. Then touched he their eyes, saying, According to your faith be it unto you. And their eyes were opened..."

- Mark 5:34, "...Daughter, thy faith hath made thee whole; go in peace, and be whole of thy plague."

This gift of healing is of no benefit if we leave it on a shelf unopened. We must take it by faith through Christ. Healing is a promise and benefit given by

God to all who trust and accept it. We must approach our healing with an attitude of boldness, saying, "If God gave it to me, I take it now!"

How to Take Your Healing

Now that we have established that it is God's will for you to be healed and walk in divine health, let's explore how you can scripturally take your healing. Jesus suffered extreme pain and punishment so that we could be restored and made whole. Let's take a look at the story of Naaman in the Bible. He was a Syrian army commander who had leprosy. In search of a cure, Naaman went to the house of the prophet Elisha. The prophet sent a messenger to him, saying: *"Go and wash yourself seven times in the Jordan River. Then your skin will be restored, and you will be healed of your leprosy" (II Kings 5:10, NLT).*

Naaman responded angrily to the request because he did not want to immerse himself in the muddy

Jordan River. It was the worst of all the rivers in Israel. However, Naaman's servants reasoned with him in II Kings 5:13 (NIV), saying: *"My father, if the prophet had told you to do some great thing, would you not have done it? How much more, then, when he tells you, 'Wash and be cleansed'!"*

Naaman emerged clean with his skin like that of a newborn baby. Many of us will react the same way when God commands us to do something we may not want to do. In our stubbornness, we negotiate with God and miss out on His best. Naaman's experience was humbling, but he arose miraculously restored.

Likewise, this same physical restoration is available to us if we submit ourselves to the will of God. As born-again believers, we are restored and receive our healing by faith in Jesus' name and His Word. We can take back by force what the enemy has stolen.

We need to take this biblical approach to scripturally take our healing despite the presence of symptoms in the form of sickness and disease: hear and be healed. The presence of symptoms in our body may be facts, but the truth of God's Word is greater and will override them every time. Many times, the root of our challenge in receiving healing is that we have a hearing deficit. Particularly, a deficit in hearing the healing promises of God so that faith can arise in our hearts to take our healing.

Every Word of God carries the ability and power of God to remove every burden and destroy every yoke (Isaiah 10:27). Our faith is the detonator that triggers the power in the Word to be released on our behalf. In the case of healing, you need to take time to hear and meditate in healing scriptures so that your mind is renewed and revelation knowledge is planted in your heart.

Biblical meditation means to dwell in thought, to contemplate, study, turn, and revolve scriptures in your mind. The meditation process also includes speaking God's Word. This is how the Word moves from being information to revelation knowledge or 'revealed knowledge' in your spirit. Revelation knowledge, not information, is the launching pad for faith. We release our faith through words, particularly by declaring and decreeing that we are healed right now in Jesus' name. Don't wait for the symptoms to leave to declare healing. Declare it now by faith!

Personal Reflection

1. It's important that you keep healing scriptures before your eyes and in your ears to keep your faith strong in this area. Write down two healing scriptures you plan to study and meditate on in the next seven days.

_____

_____

_____

_____

2. What spiritual truths about healing stood out to you in this chapter?

_____

_____

_____

_____

3. What changes in your thinking about healing do you need to make going forward?

_____

_____

_____

_____

Confession of Faith: According to 1 Peter 2:24, I declare and decree in the name of Jesus that I am healed from every form of sickness and disease!

HEALING IS YOUR
COVENANT RIGHT AS A
CHILD OF GOD.

CHAPTER THREE
Emotional Restoration

Psalm 23:3
"He restoreth my soul"

In the past decade, we have seen such a significant rise in the mental health arena. Suicide, depression, and fear have taken a toll not only among adults but our youth as well. Many individuals are just coping, trying to keep it together, and making the best of every situation. This is not the life that Jesus died for us to receive.

We have been called to live in peace. It's time to confront the issues that have been keeping us in a place of defeat. Yes, the cares of life come to each one of us but thank God we have an answer in Jesus. "Many are the afflictions of the righteous: but the Lord delivereth him out of them all" (Psalm 34:19).

God wants us strengthened emotionally and restored in our souls. The word 'restoreth,' as it appears in the original Hebrew language, in Psalm 23:3, means to rescue, recover, relieve, and refresh.[1] The Word of God carries the ability to bring your soul to a place of rest. If all you do is keep rehearsing how bad things are, you allow that problem to stay in your life. The enemy cannot do any more than what you allow.

Isaiah 61:3 tells us to put on *"the garment of praise for the spirit of heaviness."* One of the first things you do before leaving your house in the morning is to put on your clothes. In our western society, it is inappropriate for you to come out of your home naked, and so it is in the kingdom of God. There are so many Christians walking around spiritually naked and not prepared to stand against whatever they may face during the day.

We are a spirit-being possessing a soul and living in a physical body. With our spirit, we contact the spirit realm. With our bodies, we reach the physical realm. With our soul, we contact the intellectual and emotional realm. The soul is where our mind, will, and emotions are housed. This is the battleground where the enemy will try to use anything he can to distract us.

In James 1:21, we read how our souls can be delivered from trouble, *"Wherefore lay apart all filthiness and superfluity of naughtiness, and receive with meekness the engrafted word which is able to save your souls."* The Greek word for save in this passage is 'sozo,' which means deliver, protect, heal, preserve, and make whole.[2] Notice that James was writing to Christians instructing them on how their souls would be saved. It's clear in this verse that the only thing that will save the soul is the Word of God.

The word engrafted means to plant firmly; establish.[3] It is only to the degree that the Word of God is planted that your soul can remain in a place of being: delivered, protected, healed, and preserved. You cannot expect a fruit tree to grow where no seed has been planted. Every morning you should be decreeing and declaring the Word over your life.

Job 22:28 says, *"Thou shalt also decree a thing, and it shall be established unto thee: and the light shall shine upon thy ways."* God cannot establish what you fail to decree. Many Christians think they're waiting on God, but really, He's waiting on them to open their mouth and speak the Word.

Our thinking affects us emotionally, and it shows up in the choices we make every day. You can always trace negative emotions back to wrong thinking. Have you noticed the longer you think about how someone has done you wrong, the angrier you become? This is why the Bible encourages us to keep our thoughts in agreement with God. If we meditated in the promises of God more than we meditated on the problems and challenges of life, we would stabilize emotionally and walk in peace and joy.

You will find some of the greatest attacks of the enemy will come against your mind. If the enemy can get you to accept defeat, he will rob you of the victory that already belongs to you. The way you think will impact what you believe and how you see yourself. When thoughts of worry, fear, and doubt come to you, address that lie of the enemy by declaring a scripture that speaks of your victory in that area.

We are transformed by renewing our minds. God desires that our will - the part of our souls that allows us the freedom to decide - aligns with Him in all things. Oftentimes, the paths we choose are not the ones God chose for us. Our human desires can sometimes run contrary to God's commands. The abundant life God desires to provide for us includes a strong spirit, renewed mind, restored emotions, and a surrendered will.

Let's establish what did and did not happen at salvation when we accepted Jesus as our personal Lord and Savior. II Corinthians 5:17 says, *"Therefore if any man be in Christ, he is a new creature: old things are passed away; behold all things are become new."* This leads us to ask, "What became new?" It was our spirit man that was made new with the nature of God. The old sin nature is gone. With this in mind, two things did not change when we got saved: 1) our body; and 2) our soul (mind, will, and emotions).

Have you noticed that since you got saved, you haven't forgotten how to curse, lie, steal, etc.? Why?

Because your heart was transformed, but your flesh must be disciplined. Oftentimes when certain individuals come with drama, you have to remind yourself to not respond in the flesh. The enemy will use people to get us off track and distracted from where God is trying to take us.

Paul wrote to the believers at the church in Rome admonishing them on what to do with their body and soul. Let's take a look at Romans 12:1-2, *"I beseech you therefore, brethren, by the mercies of God, that ye present your bodies a living sacrifice, holy, acceptable unto God, which is your reasonable service. And be not conformed to this world: but be ye transformed by the renewing of your mind, that ye may prove what is that good, and acceptable, and perfect will of God."* God's Word helps us to renew our minds with what is true, honest, just, pure, lovely, and of a good report (Philippians 4:8).

II Corinthians 10:5 says, *"casting down imaginations,*

and every high thing that exalteth itself against the knowledge of God, and bringing into captivity every thought to the obedience of Christ." Casting down imaginations is an intentional action that must be done daily. There are always going to be a million reasons why you can't move forward, why you can't be successful, and why you can't make it. If you don't learn how to address those thoughts, you will be limited in how far you go in your destiny.

Your spiritual diet is going to determine your progress in the things of God. What you eat or fail to eat consistently will show up in your soul (mind, will, and emotions). In the natural, if you want to change your health and quality of life, you must first examine the foods you are eating. Likewise, the transformation of your soul starts with the transformation of your spiritual diet.

The more time you spend fellowshipping with God,

the stronger your spirit will become. Proverbs 18:14 (AMPC) says, *"The strong spirit of a man sustains him in bodily pain or trouble, but a weak and broken spirit who can raise up or bear?"* We fellowship with God in three ways: 1) Prayer, 2) Word of God, and 3) Worship. Let's stay in close communion with Him as He prepares to reveal more of His plans to us.

Personal Reflection

1. The scripture admonishes us in Proverbs 4:23 and John 14:1 to guard our hearts and not allow our hearts to be troubled. What has been troubling your mind and heart? Find a scripture in the Word of God that answers it with a promise of God.

   _____

   _____

   _____

   _____

   _____

2. We fellowship with God in three ways: 1) Prayer, 2) Word of God, and 3) Worship. In what areas do you need to spend more time with Him? Write out a plan on how you will adjust your schedule to accomplish this.

   _____

_____

_____

_____

_____

_____

3. What spiritual truth stood out to you in this chapter?

_____

_____

_____

_____

_____

Confession: I declare and decree in the name of Jesus that my mind, will, and emotions are restored. I am not ruled by anything except the Word of God. Depression and stress cannot overtake me!

"

IT IS ONLY TO THE DEGREE
THAT THE WORD OF GOD IS
ENGRAFTED IN YOU THAT
YOUR SOUL IS DELIVERED,
PROTECTED, HEALED,
PRESERVED, AND MADE
WHOLE.

"

CHAPTER FOUR
Financial Restoration

Psalm 23:1, NLT
"The Lord is my shepherd; I have all that I need."

As heirs to His promise, God is positioning us to be financially restored so that we may fulfill our God-given assignments on the earth, spread the message of the Gospel, and build the kingdom for His glory. God wants us to flourish in every area of our life. He assures us in His Word that He will provide everything we need, including financial resources, to accomplish the will of God on the earth.

The needs in the Body of Christ are vast, and resources are necessary to ensure they are met. We need people in our churches who can write checks for mission trips, randomly pay school tuition for children who can't afford it, and purchase vehicles to transport our youth to church outings and excursions. God wants to bless us so that we can be a blessing. He is the unfailing, unlimited source of our supply, and we will not lack anything.

He is our provider, and it is His great pleasure to prosper us. Financial restoration demands that everything lost or taken from us is returned. This means we will have more than enough to fulfill our kingdom assignments and bless those around us, including our elders, widows, and children. Deuteronomy 28:12-13 provides for us a vision of the blessed life God is preparing for us: *"...and thou shalt lend unto many nations, and thou shalt not borrow. And the Lord shall make thee the head, and not the tail; and thou shalt be above only, and thou shalt not be beneath."*

While our reason for serving God must never be to obtain material wealth, God wants to provide for us so that we are in a position to be a blessing. The Lord is well able to open to us His good treasure and bless the works of our hands. When we obey God, He promises to transform and bless us in the city and the field.

Gathering the Spoils

"And when Jehoshaphat and his people came to take away the spoil of them, they found among them in abundance both riches with the dead bodies, and precious jewels, which they stripped off for themselves, more than they could carry away: and they were three days in gathering of the spoil, it was so much." II Chronicles 20:25

In the days of King Jehoshaphat, the people of Israel exercised unwavering faith when three nations joined forces to invade their country. Jehoshaphat, the fourth king of Judah, was one of the few God-fearing kings of his time. He destroyed the sites of idol worshippers, restored the temple, and set in motion the law of Moses as a standard by which the people lived. When the armies joined forces to attack Israel, King Jehoshaphat's response was unlike that of any other king in Israel.

He assembled the entire nation, and they began to pray. In the natural, they were powerless against the combined armies, but in the spirit, they were more powerful than all of the armies arrayed against them. When Jehoshaphat's soldiers went out to meet the army of invaders, they found corpses because the invading militias had turned on each other and destroyed themselves.

God honored Jehoshaphat's faithfulness and protected the king and Israelites from their enemies. The scripture confirms in II Chronicles 20:25, that when King Jehoshaphat and his people went out to plunder the war zone, they began collecting the riches and treasure of the fallen armies. It took three days to gather all of the spoils. Their win is a testament to the power of God to use unlikely and unforeseen situations to shower His people with abundance and financial overflow.

Likewise, God is setting us up to gather spoils and reap an unplanned harvest. It is His reward to us for our faithfulness, diligence, and consistency. All that the enemy has stolen from us is returning seven-fold. When King Jehoshaphat and the Israelites returned to Jerusalem after defeating their enemies, the news of this miraculous victory spread to surrounding kingdoms. We don't know who or what God will use to bless us, but we must remember it is our duty to give back to God a portion of what He so generously gives to us.

Seedtime & Harvest

"While the earth remaineth, seedtime and harvest, and cold and heat, and summer and winter, and day and night shall not cease." Genesis 8:22

A harvest can only be reaped if seeds are sown. In the body of Christ, our seeds are our tithes and offerings. We plant them in good ground, and when the rain comes, it produces a harvest. An overflowing harvest is coming, and our storehouses will be full.

This law holds true in both the natural and spiritual realms. The concept of seedtime and harvest, as declared in scripture, is as certain as day and night. The harvest a farmer yields has everything to do with crop selection, land preparation, seed selection, seed sowing, irrigation, crop growth, fertilization, and harvesting. Every step in the process of the farming life cycle is essential to success. Likewise, for us to experience the fullness of God's grace and reap the harvest He intends for us, we must take the necessary steps to ensure a plentiful yield. Like farmers, we must:

- Be selective of the crops and seeds we sow.

Not all seeds are created equal because some are superior while others are inferior. Superior seeds will always yield healthy crops and a bountiful harvest. These high-quality seeds represent our diligent walk with God, regular study of His Word, and our obedience in tithes and offerings.

- Inferior seeds yield a subpar harvest. We must weed out low-grade seeds like doubt, fear, and unbelief, which weakens the strength of the harvest God intended. The seeds we sow dictate the success or failure of our harvest. When we sow low, we reap below. The seeds we plant must be nurtured and supported by the Word of God, faith, prayer, and fasting.

- Discern the best ground to plant our seeds. The presence of God sanctifies the land, and His blessing purifies it from diseases that could destroy the harvest He intends for us to reap. The blessing of the Lord balances the ground by stabilizing its fertility to absorb the water and nutrients essential for growth. Expect a harvest on every seed you have sown.

God Is Our Source & Provider

"No one can serve two masters. Either you will hate the one and love the other, or you will be devoted to the one and despise the other. You cannot serve both God and money." Matthew 6:24, NIV

We must rely on God to be our source and provider. The Bible reminds us in Deuteronomy 8:18 that it is the Lord who gives us the power to get wealth. It is not the money that destroys men and women of faith but the love of money that causes us to fall from grace. The scripture cautions us in I Timothy 6:10 that, *"...the love of money is the root of all evil: which while some coveted after, they have erred from the faith, and pierced themselves through with many sorrows."*

When we worship or idolize money over God, we position ourselves in a dangerous place. We must remember that we are on assignment for Christ, and the provision will help us fulfill the Great Commission. We must be equipped and prepared to carry out our assignments without the hindrances of poverty and lack. The enemy will try and cause you to run out of time and resources before you reach the end of your assignment. We declare that we will be on time with a full supply for every heavenly assignment!

Personal Reflection

1. What spiritual truth stood out to you in this chapter?

_____

_____

_____

_____

2. How can you be more faithful as a steward over the finances God has already entrusted to you?

_____

_____

_____

_____

3. Are there any areas in your life where your trust has shifted from God to money?

Confession of Faith: I declare and decree in the name of Jesus that all my needs are met. My finances are restored, and I will fulfill my God-given assignments.

"

AS HEIRS TO HIS PROMISE,
GOD IS POSITIONING US TO
BE FINANCIALLY RESTORED
SO THAT WE MAY FULFILL
OUR GOD-GIVEN
ASSIGNMENTS ON THE
EARTH.

"

CHAPTER FIVE
Spiritual Restoration: The Fruit of the Spirit

Joel 2:28-29, NLT

"Then, after doing all those things, I will pour out my Spirit upon all people. Your sons and daughters will prophesy. Your old men will dream dreams, and your young men will see visions. In those days, I will pour out my Spirit even on servants—men and women alike."

God desires to move us to a place in Him where the fruit and gifts of the Spirit are evident, alive, and active in our lives. In this chapter, we will explore the nine fruits of the spirit and their role in perfecting us so that we look and sound like Christ on the earth. He is the head of the church, and we are His body. He desires to manifest His glory in and through us to a lost and dying world. When we take the time to develop in the fruit of the spirit, we are growing in godly character and exuding the love and nature of God.

Let's take a look at Galatians 5:18-24:

"But if ye be led of the Spirit, ye are not under the law. Now the works of the flesh are manifest, which are these; Adultery, fornication, uncleanness, lasciviousness, idolatry, witchcraft, hatred, variance, emulations, wrath, strife, seditions, heresies, envyings, murders, drunkenness, revellings, and such like: of the which I tell you before, as I have also told you in time past, that they which do such things shall not inherit the kingdom of God. But the fruit of the Spirit is love, joy, peace, longsuffering, gentleness, goodness, faith, meekness, temperance: against such there is no law. And they that are Christ's have crucified the flesh with the affections and lusts."

Our flesh produces works, but our spirit produces fruit. Many times, what we have attributed to the devil was nothing more than the manifestation of a work of our flesh. This is why Paul admonishes us in Romans 12:1 (AMPC) to do the following, *"…make a decisive dedication of your bodies [presenting all your members and faculties] as a living sacrifice, holy (devoted, consecrated) and well-pleasing to God, which is your reasonable (rational, intelligent) service and spiritual worship."* Notice that making a decisive dedication of our bodies to the lordship of Christ and His Word is crucifying the flesh, which is a part of our 'spiritual worship.'

The fruit of the spirit is the fruit of your recreated spirit. Just like fruit on a tree, it can be cultivated and developed when we give it proper attention and the necessary nourishment. Have you ever seen fruit on a tree that wasn't fully developed? It was in an infantile stage in its growth and development. Likewise, if we don't give proper attention and the necessary nourishment to the nine fruits of the spirit, they will be dormant or not fully developed in our spiritual walk.

I believe, according to scripture, love is at the root of the eight fruits of the spirit, which means they grow and flourish out of the love of God that has been shed abroad in our hearts according to Romans 5:5. The Holy Spirit guides us into truth by directing us down paths that help us to be more like God. Remember, the scriptures say that God is love. When we allow God to lead and guide us, we activate and display His nature.

Love

This word in the Greek language is agape which means it is divine love. God is love, and love itself is the greatest gift of all. When we choose to love, harmony is the result. We can see each other as God sees us and extend unconditional compassion to those around us. The God-kind of love is clearly defined in I Corinthians 13:4-8 (AMPC). I encourage you to make this your daily confession of faith:

"I endure long, and I am patient and kind. I am never envious, nor do I boil over with jealousy. I am not boastful or vainglorious. I do not display myself haughtily. I am not

conceited, arrogant, and inflated with pride. I am not rude, and I do not act unbecomingly. I do not insist on my own rights or my own way. I am not self-seeking. I am not touchy, fretful, or resentful. I take no account of the evil done to me. I pay no attention to a suffered wrong. I do not rejoice at injustice and unrighteousness, but I rejoice when right and truth prevail. The love of God in me bears up under anything and everything that comes. I am ever ready to believe the best of every person. Love's hopes are fadeless under all circumstances, and it endures everything without weakening. Love never fails!"

Joy

It's important to note that joy and happiness are not the same thing. Happiness is based on external circumstances, while joy is a spiritual force based on the integrity and efficacy of God's infallible Word and character, which never changes. Nehemiah 8:10 says the joy of the Lord is our strength!

Peace

God gives us peace that surpasses understanding. This means we can be at rest, even when turmoil is at work all around us. We can operate in wholeness and completeness because outer circumstances will not affect this inner peace.

Longsuffering

God strengthens our hearts and builds calmness and steadfastness in us when we wait on Him. We don't need to be anxious for anything because the promises of God are yes and amen. I Corinthians 15:58 reminds us to, *"...be ye stedfast, unmoveable, always abounding in the work of the Lord, forasmuch as ye know that your labour is not in vain in the Lord."*

Gentleness

Our willingness to be helpful to others around us is restoration in action. We have the heart to show and extend kindness to everyone. We must imitate Him by loving our neighbors, doing good, and expecting nothing in return. God will restore and make our reward great!

Goodness

The very nature of God is good. Romans 2:4 says, *"...the goodness of God leadeth thee to repentance."* When we develop in this fruit, we extend benevolence to others.

Faith

God's faithfulness is great toward us! There is always a reward on the other side of our faithfulness to God and His plan for our lives. Matthew 25:23 says, *"... Well done, good and faithful servant; thou hast been faithful over a few things, I will make thee ruler over many things: enter thou into the joy of thy lord."*

Meekness

Meekness is not to be considered a display of

weakness. It means that you have a teachable and humble spirit before the Lord. We can see this highlighted in I Peter 3:4, which references a meek and quiet spirit. It means to not be anxious, agitated, or wrought about anything but rather at peace looking unto God, who is the author and finisher of our faith.

I Peter 5:5 says that God resists the proud but gives grace to the humble. To be humble means that you have surrendered your will, motives, intentions, and way to the Lord. It means that you have decided to yield to His leading and counsel in all things. There is a supernatural grace that is released in the lives of those who walk in humility.

Temperance

Temperance is self-control and discipline. It's the cultivation of walking in the spirit and not fulfilling the works of the flesh. It's a steady and consistent pace in God that does not exhibit lasciviousness or a lack of restraint in word and deed.

When the fruit of the spirit is at work, godly character is evident. It manifests in the way we carry ourselves and interact with family and friends. We position ourselves to reap a harvest of benefits we could not realize on our own. Walking in the fruit of the spirit assures us that we will bring forth fruit that will remain.

Personal Reflection

1. Which fruits of the spirit do you need to grow and develop in?

_____

_____

_____

_____

_____

2. Select one of the fruits of the spirit you need to grow and list all of the practical ways you can express this fruit in a greater way daily.

_____

_____

_____

_____

_____

3. In what areas of your life have you been operating

in pride instead of humility? How can you yield to the leading of God's Word and His Spirit in this area?

_____

_____

_____

_____

_____

Confession of Faith: I walk in love, joy, peace, longsuffering, gentleness, goodness, faith, meekness, and temperance!

OUR FLESH PRODUCES
WORKS, BUT OUR SPIRIT
PRODUCES FRUIT.

CHAPTER SIX
Spiritual Restoration: The Gifts of the Spirit

I Corinthians 12:1, 7-11

"Now concerning spiritual gifts, brethren, I would not have you ignorant. But the manifestation of the Spirit is given to every man to profit withal. For to one is given by the Spirit the word of wisdom; to another the word of knowledge by the same Spirit; to another faith by the same Spirit; to another the gifts of healing by the same Spirit; to another the working of miracles; to another prophecy; to another discerning of spirits; to another divers kinds of tongues: to another the interpretation of tongues; But all these worketh that one and the self-same Spirit, dividing to every man severally as he will."

We are living in a time where the world is in search of supernatural power. There has been such a rise in spiritual practices, false religions, and idol worship. Men are in search of power that is beyond their ability to help them cope with the challenges of life. This is the finest hour for the body of Christ to yield to the Spirit of God and demonstrate the power of God.

Jesus told the disciples upon His ascension in Luke 24:49 (NIV), *"...but stay in the city until you have been clothed with power from on high."* There was a deeper dimension of the Spirit that was necessary for each one of them to fulfill their assignment in God. Isn't it interesting that Jesus would not release them into their ministry without the power of the Holy Spirit? Even Jesus Himself did not step into His earthly ministry without first being full of the Spirit (Luke 4:1).

In Acts 2:4, after the 120 disciples were all filled with the Holy Ghost, we see them begin to function in miracles, signs, and wonders. The book of Acts is a book of the demonstrations of the Holy Spirit. We can see why Jesus didn't want the early Church to begin without this power. Even as it relates to us today, we cannot follow in the footsteps of Jesus and do the same works and even greater without the Holy Spirit.

The time has come for a restoration of the gifts of the Spirit among the Church. Miracles were not just for previous generations to experience; they are for us as well. As we spend time in prayer and consecration before the Lord, His Spirit will begin to move upon us in our churches, homes, and marketplace. God is looking for someone who will position themselves to be used in the realm of the supernatural.

Notice that Paul's writing to the church at Corinth admonished them to not be ignorant regarding the gifts of the Spirit. When the gifts of the Spirit are in manifestation, they will glorify God. I Corinthians 12:3 says, *"…no man speaking by the Spirit of God calleth Jesus accursed; and that no man can say that Jesus is the Lord, but by the Holy Ghost."*

What are the gifts of the Spirit? Simply put, it's the way the Spirit of God chooses to manifest Himself. The reason why God had Paul outline what these manifestations are is so we could identify these supernatural workings of God from the ordinary works of men. They are called gifts because the Spirit works through believers as He wills. They are given to profit or help us in the body of Christ, but they do not belong to any one person. You cannot choose to operate in these supernatural works as you will; they require His prompting. As we define the nine gifts of the Spirit, it would be helpful for us to divide them into the following categories.

The Revelation Gifts
Gifts That Reveal Something

- **Word of Knowledge:** The gift of the word of knowledge is not to be confused with natural knowledge because it is a supernatural manifestation of the Spirit of God, not our intellect. We must remember that none of the gifts of the Spirit are natural, but they are all supernatural. Word of knowledge is a supernatural revelation by the Spirit of God of certain facts in the mind of God that He wants to reveal to us or others. Notice, it is a word, a piece, or fragment of information from the whole counsel or knowledge of God. This gift will reveal details of the past or present concerning a person, place, or thing.

Let's look at a biblical example of this gift in manifestation in the New Testament. The Lord appeared in a vision to Ananias revealing this to him concerning Saul in Acts 9:11-12, *"... Arise, and go into the street which is called Straight, and enquire in the house of Judas for one called Saul of Tarsus: for, behold he prayeth, and hath seen in a vision a man named Ananias coming in, and putting his hand on him, that he might receive his sight."*

There was no way in the natural that Ananias
could have known that Saul was praying and
had a vision seeing him lay hands on him
to receive his sight. No one had stopped by
Ananias' home to report what Jesus had
spoken to Saul in a vision. Ananias knew
this by the manifestation of the word of
knowledge.

- **Word of Wisdom:** Word of wisdom is a
supernatural revelation by the Spirit of God
of the plans and purposes of God in the
future. Let's look at this gift in manifestation
through the prophet Agabus in Acts 21:10-11,
*"And as we tarried there many days, there came down
from Judaea a certain prophet named Agabus. And
when he was come unto us, he took Paul's girdle, and
bound his own hands and feet, and said, Thus saith
the Holy Ghost, So shall the Jews at Jerusalem bind
the man that owneth this girdle, and shall deliver him*

into the hands of the Gentiles. " Agabus shared by
the Spirit of God something that was going to
happen in the future. The difference between
this gift and prophecy is that the word of
wisdom reveals what will happen in the future.
The gift of prophecy has more to do with
God's intention for the future; however, it can
be altered by the decisions of man. Prophecy
reveals what God wants to do.

• **Discerning of Spirits:** This gift is the
ability to see and hear in the spiritual realm.
This is inclusive of angels and evil spirits. It
is not the discernment of character flaws or
the criticism of others, but it allows you to
step over into the supernatural world. We see
an example of this with Zacharias (John the
Baptist's father) in Luke 1:11-13 *"And there
appeared unto him an angel of the Lord standing
on the right side of the altar of incense. And when*

Zacharias saw him, he was troubled, and fear fell upon him. But the angel said unto him, Fear not, Zacharias: for thy prayer is heard; and thy wife Elisabeth shall bear thee a son, and thou shalt call his name John." The Holy Spirit opened the eyes of Zacharias not only to see but to hear the angel in the spirit realm. You can also see this gift manifest when casting out an evil spirit.

The Power Gifts
Gifts That Do Something

- **Gift of Faith:** This is a manifestation of special faith to step into the miraculous and receive a miracle. This is not the same as general faith, which is believing God for your needs to be met according to the Word of God. The Holy Spirit endows you with a holy boldness to go beyond the natural. We can see this in operation when Jesus raised

Lazarus from the dead. John 11:43-44 says, *"And when he thus had spoken, he cried with a loud voice, Lazarus, come forth. And he that was dead came forth, bound hand and foot with graveclothes: and his face was bound about with a napkin. Jesus saith unto them, Loose him, and let him go."* The Spirit of God was at work through Jesus to command death to lose its hold on Lazarus' body.

- **Working of Miracles:** This manifestation is given to a believer to perform a miracle. We see countless examples of this gift in operation in both the Old and New Testament from blind eyes being opened, deaf ears hearing again, Jesus turning water into wine, etc. There was one example of an ax being retrieved from the water in II Kings 6:5-7 *"But as one was felling a beam, the axe head fell into the water: and he cried, and said, Alas, master! for it was borrowed. And the man of God said, Where fell it? And he* *shewed him the place. And he cut down a stick, and cast it in thither; and the iron did swim. Therefore said he, Take it up to thee. And he put out his hand, and took it."*

- **Gifts of Healings:** This is a supernatural intervention of healing from a sickness, disease, or ailment. This manifestation of the Spirit is not to be confused with a person receiving healing on their faith based on God's Word. You can receive healing at any time without a gift of the Spirit because this is our divine right as a child of God to be healed. God is so merciful and gracious to those that might not have the faith or the knowledge of healing that His Spirit will intervene in those cases.

We can see in the ministry of Jesus how certain individuals were healed because they believed and others were healed through God's mercy.

John 5:5-9 says, *"And a certain man was there, which had an infirmity thirty and eight years. When Jesus saw him lie, and knew that he had been now a long time in that case, he saith unto him, Wilt thou be made whole? The impotent man answered him, Sir, I have no man, when the water is troubled, to put me into the pool: but while I am coming, another steppeth down before me. Jesus saith unto him, Rise, take up thy bed, and walk. And immediately the man was made whole, and took up his bed, and walked: and on the same day was the sabbath."*

The Utterance Gifts
Gifts That Say Something

- **Prophecy:** This is a supernatural utterance in our known tongue that reveals God's intentions for the future; it also oftentimes comes with instructions. When a prophecy is given, it becomes the job of the recipient to adhere and adjust to what God is saying. I Corinthians 14:3 says, *"…he that prophesieth speaketh unto men to edification, and exhortation and comfort."* Prophecy will always confirm what is in your heart. It may also bring warning and correction; however, the intention is never to embarrass or demean but to help.

- **Divers Kinds of Tongues:** This is a supernatural utterance in an unknown tongue, not necessarily unknown to mankind but unknown to you. We see an example of this on the day of Pentecost in Acts 2:7-8 *"And they were all amazed and marvelled, saying one to another, Behold, are not all these which speak Galilæans? And how hear we every man in our own tongue, wherein we were born?"* The Spirit of God caused the 120 disciples to speak a language they had not learned nor rehearsed. This gift is also used in giving a message of the Spirit and is often coupled with an interpretation.

- **Interpretation of Tongues:** This is the interpretation of the meaning that was said in an unknown tongue. It is not a word-for-word translation but rather an interpretation. This is why a message in tongues could be very long but the interpretation short because it is not a translation.

What a tremendous aid these gifts are to the body of Christ. We must never forget that these gifts are not for personal gratification, but they are a testament to God's power. If the Spirit of God chooses to use someone in these gifts, it does not make them more spiritual or more important. These supernatural gifts and abilities are given to believers as they yield themselves to the Holy Spirit.

It's time to get interested in what God is doing on the

earth in the end of days. He is looking to manifest His glory and power through you on the earth, so take time in prayer and consecration before the Lord in His presence. Will you answer the call of God today? Isaiah 6:8 *"Also I heard the voice of the Lord, saying, Whom shall I send? And who will go for Us? Then said I, Here am I; send me."*

Personal Reflection

1. What did you learn about the gifts of the Spirit that you didn't know before?

_____

_____

_____

_____

_____

2. How can we remain humble when God uses us in the gifts of the Spirit?

_____

_____

_____

_____

_____

3. What spiritual truth stood out to you in this chapter?

_____

_____

_____

_____

_____

Confession of Faith: I will always give God the glory and honor whenever He manifests a gift of the Spirit through me.

"

IT'S TIME TO GET
INTERESTED IN WHAT GOD
IS DOING ON THE EARTH IN
THESE LAST DAYS. HE IS
LOOKING TO MANIFEST HIS
GLORY AND POWER
THROUGH YOU ON THE
EARTH!

"

CHAPTER SEVEN
Training Our Youth in the Ways of God

Daniel 1:3 MSG
*"The king told Ashpenaz, head of the palace staff, to get some
Israelites from the royal family and nobility—young men who were
healthy and handsome, intelligent and well-educated, good prospects
for leadership positions in the government, perfect specimens!—and
indoctrinate them in the Babylonian language and the lore of magic
and fortunetelling"*

God wants to dispense a greater anointing on our
children so that they are an effective witness of His
glory and love. It is our responsibility to raise our
children in the nurture and admonition of God so
that we may establish a generational legacy of faith.
It's important that spiritual truths and revelations
from the Word of God are not lost to this generation.
We have seen a departure from doctrinal teachings
on faith, healing, prayer, being led by the Spirit of

God, renewing the mind, gifts of the Spirit, etc., amongst this generation. If we don't impart these revelations to our children, a generation will grow up not knowing God.

Notice what Moses told the children of Israel in Deuteronomy 6:1-2 (NLT), *"These are the commands, decrees, and regulations that the Lord your God commanded me to teach you. You must obey them in the land you are about to enter and occupy, and you and your children and grandchildren must fear the Lord your God as long as you live."*

The scripture further assures the children of Israel that long life is the reward for obedience. Moses insisted that the Israelites talk with their children daily about God's law in the home. We are responsible for the spiritual growth of our children, not a pastor or church. One day they will leave our homes and be spiritually tested. They must be able to effectively apply what we have taught them about the Word of God.

If we don't pour the Word of God into our children, they are going to surrender to worldly influences. We want our children to be well-rounded and enjoy their youth, but not at the expense of being spiritually bankrupt. We must pray with our youth, show them how to meditate in God's Word, and grow spiritually.

The scripture tells us in Deuteronomy 6:8-9 how the Israelites tied the laws of God to their finger, wore it on their forehead, and wrote it on the doorposts of their homes. These practices today would seem bizarre, but the Pharisees in Jesus' day took this spiritual practice seriously. They created and wore small leather boxes containing commandments and scriptures as a reminder to keep the law. What's more, Jewish people wrote the law on the doorposts and outer gates of their homes. Although these practices seem extreme today, we must ensure that God's Word is deeply rooted in the hearts and minds of our youth.

An article published in The International Network of Children's Ministries titled, "Why Children Are the Most Important People in the Church" helps us to understand the importance of guiding our youth to greater truth and a strong relationship with Jesus Christ. Damon DeLillo points out in the article these important facts:

- "Nearly 80% of people in our churches today decided to follow Jesus before age 18. 50% of them decided to follow Jesus before age 12. In fact, it becomes exponentially rarer and exponentially harder for a person to decide to follow Christ after age 18."

- "There is a season in a person's life when they

are most open to learning what it means to trust God. It's a season — sometime between ages 4-14 — when people are more moldable than they will ever be in their lifetime. It's when people are forming their understanding of the world, of relationships, of love, of God. It's a season when people are impressionable. We should be intentional about ensuring that they get the right impression. What is rooted in the heart of a child is almost impossible to uproot in the life of an adult. Many people call this the 4–14 Window. What we do during this window may be the most important thing the church does."[1]

Damon DeLillo's article affirms that we are living in a time when many churches do not have functional youth and children's ministries. Unfortunately, the attention at many churches is on the adults only. Our children are left to find their way without the benefit of spiritual impartation or guidance from an adult. This next generation will be the kingdom's future preachers, teachers, leaders, and missionaries.

We are commanded by God in Proverbs 22:6 to *"train up a child in the way he should go: and when he is old, he will not depart from it."* Train means to coach, drill, guide, mold, shape, sharpen, and qualify. We must qualify and prepare our children to have a personal relationship with God and fulfill their God-given purpose on the earth.

Protecting Our Youth From Worldly Influences

"The king told Ashpenaz, head of the palace staff, to get some Israelites from the royal family and nobility—young men who were healthy and handsome, intelligent and well-educated, good prospects for leadership positions in the government, perfect specimens!—and indoctrinate them in the Babylonian language and the lore of magic and fortunetelling"

Daniel 1:3, MSG.

As we guide our youth toward their destiny, the world is competing to turn them against the laws of God. Our focus must be on protecting them from the world's influences and positioning them to stand on God's Word. The book of Daniel gives us a roadmap of how God prevails with us when the world seeks to make us conform to their rules and customs. The story of Daniel and his friends, Shadrach, Meshach, and Abednego, begins when Babylon defeats Judah. It was customary for the victors of war to remove the leaders and most promising young people out of a defeated country to prevent an uprising.

King Nebuchadnezzar ordered Ashpenaz, head of the palace personnel, to select the most exceptional young men from the captives to train in the Chaldean language and culture. Ashpenaz chose Daniel, Shadrach, Meshach, and Abednego. King

Nebuchadnezzar provided them with choice food and wine from his kitchen, but Daniel refused the king's selection. Instead of being defiled by the king's food, Daniel convinced the warden to allow them to eat a special diet for ten days. The warden could see that Daniel, Shadrach, Meshach, and Abednego looked healthier than those who ate the king's rich food. Furthermore, the king found the young men ten times smarter than the magicians, sorcerers, and astrologers of Babylon.

The enemy always seeks out the best and brightest of our children to destroy their lives and prevent them from coming into a relationship with God. These destructive forces show up in three major areas of our children's lives. These 'plated' forces include:

The Peer Pressure Plate: So-called friends serve our children a plate of food called pressure. These frenemies pressure our children to do things that are anti-Christ. These are activities and behaviors that are contrary and in opposition to the Word and plans of God. Many of our youth have a strong desire to be liked and accepted by their peers and cave into the pressures of this world.

The Entertainment Plate: There are positive and biblically-based movies, music, and television that can positively inspire our children. Still, the power of negative entertainment and media can influence our children's behavior and draw them away from the things of God. This plate consists of extreme behaviors that foster violence, disrespect, and profanity.

The Social Media Plate: Our youth now have access to social media applications, platforms, and portals that expose them to bullying, sexual predators, secret sins, mental pollution, and so many other dangers. God has prepared for our children a table of restoration in the presence of their enemy's tactics and negative influences. God's omnipotent power can destroy any hindrances blocking this life-sustaining path that He has destined for them. They will be equipped to move into their destiny full of the knowledge of God and totally restored.

We must impart the knowledge of God and His Word into our children, lest they be separated from His love, goodness, and restoration!

Personal Reflection

1. How are you imparting a legacy of faith to your children and youth in your sphere of influence?

_____

_____

_____

_____

_____

2. How was your life impacted by the presence or absence of godly examples to impart the wisdom of God to you?

_____

_____

_____

_____

_____

3. There is power in the Word of God! Write down two scriptures that you can incorporate in

your daily confession of faith over your children.

_____

_____

_____

_____

_____

Confession of Faith: I declare and decree in the name of Jesus that I will keep the Word of God in my home and in front of my children. I will cover them in prayer daily and believe the Spirit of God will lead and guide them in the paths of righteousness.

" GOD WANTS TO DISPENSE A GREATER ANOINTING ON OUR CHILDREN SO THAT THEY ARE AN EFFECTIVE WITNESS OF HIS GLORY AND LOVE. "

Pastor T.J. McBride

T.J. McBride is the Senior Pastor of Tabernacle of Praise Church International, one of the fastest-growing congregations in McDonough and Jonesboro, Georgia. He is a community-centered trailblazer and internationally sought-after thought-leader, speaker, recording artist, and author. Pastor McBride's message and mantra are one of faith, and his ministry is the manifestation and evidence of hope.

As an author, Pastor McBride's books include: *It's According to Your Faith*; *Faith for Provision*; and *Keep Fighting*. These books are among the volumes he has written that speak to the confident assurance believers must have to win in faith. His faith has catapulted him to launch two church locations in McDonough and Jonesboro with thousands of parishioners, a Bible Institute, an early learning center, and a Christian Academy.

Pastor McBride shares his message of faith globally through outreach missions and media platforms. His *Winning in Faith* broadcast has reached millions of viewers via television and social media. Pastor McBride leads a global missions-dedicated ministry. His outreach has also taken him to Africa to give humanitarian aid, help build churches, and teach the word of faith.

Pastor T.J. is married to his wife and partner in ministry, Shunnae McBride, and together they have three children: Ashli, Andrew, and Alexis.

Salvation Prayer

Jesus, I believe that you are the Son of God and that you were sent to die for my sins. I believe that you died on the cross of Calvary and arose on the third day. The punishment you endured was my fate. I confess with my mouth and believe in my heart that God raised you from the dead. Lord Jesus, come into my heart and change my life. I surrender all that I am to you. Be the Lord over my life. Thank you for your blood that has cleansed me of all my wrong. I accept you as being my Savior, and right now, I am born again.

Notes

Chapter 1

1. restoration. (n.d.) American Heritage © Dictionary of the English Language, Fifth Edition. (2011). Retrieved September 1, 2021, from https://www.thefreedictionary.com/restoration

Chapter 3

1. James Strong, A Concise Dictionary of the Words in The Hebrew Bible. Chattanooga: AMG Publishers, 1991), 113.

2. James Strong, A Concise Dictionary of the Words in The Greek Testament. Chattanooga: AMG Publishers, 1991), 70.

3. engrafted. (n.d.) American Heritage © Dictionary of the English Language, Fifth Edition. (2011). Retrieved September 1, 2021, from https://www.thefreedictionary.com/engrafted

Chapter 7

1. Damon DeLillo. "Why Children Are the Most Important People in the Church." International Network of Children's Ministry" International Network of Children's Ministry, March 1, 2012, https://incm.wpenguine.com/why-children-are-the-most-important-people-in-the-church-everything-you-wish-your-senior-pastor-knew-about-childrens-ministry/(accessed September 1, 2021)

CPSIA information can be obtained
at www.ICGtesting.com
Printed in the USA
LVHW041031151121
703348LV00006B/164